W9-AQV-615

**Date: 12/20/12**

**J 597.35 ZEI
Zeiger, Jennifer.
Stingrays /**

PALM BEACH COUNTY
LIBRARY SYSTEM
3650 SUMMIT BLVD.
WEST PALM BEACH, FL 33406

NATURE'S CHILDREN

# STINGRAYS

*by Jennifer Zeiger*

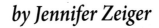

**Children's Press®**

An Imprint of Scholastic Inc.
New York   Toronto   London   Auckland   Sydney
Mexico City   New Delhi   Hong Kong
Danbury, Connecticut

Content Consultant
Dr. Stephen S. Ditchkoff
Professor of Wildlife Sciences
Auburn University
Auburn, Alabama

Photographs © 2013: Alamy Images: 11 (Dray van Beeck), 27 (Jeff
Rotman), 5 top, 20 (Mark Conlin); AP Images: 5 bottom, 39 (Courtesy
of Zeb Hogan, University of Nevada-Reno), 40 (Dino Vournas/
PRNewsPhoto/Six Flags, Inc.); Art Resource/The Metropolitan
Museum of Art: 28 (Gift of Faith-dorian and Martin Wright Family, in
memory of Douglas Newton, 2003); Bob Italiano: 44 foreground,
45 foreground; Corbis Images/Paul Souders: 4, 5 background, 7;
Dreamstime/Tatiana Belova: 2 background, 3, 44 background, 45
background; Getty Images: 31 (Andy Murch/Visuals Unlimited, Inc.),
15 (Paul Kay), cover (Stephen Frink); iStockphoto/Edwin van Wier:
23; National Geographic Stock/Ralph Lee Hopkins: 32; Nature
Picture Library: 12 (Alex Mustard), 24 (Georgette Douwma), 36 (Jeff
Rotman); Seapics.com: 35; Shutterstock, Inc.: 1, 2 foreground, 46
(Brad Thompson), 8 (Konoka Amane), 19 (Stephen Kerkhofs), 16
(worldswildlifewonders).

Library of Congress Cataloging-in-Publication Data
Zeiger, Jennifer.
  Stingrays/by Jennifer Zeiger.
    p. cm.—(Nature's children)
  Includes bibliographical references and index.
  ISBN-13: 978-0-531-26838-4 (lib. bdg.)
  ISBN-13: 978-0-531-25483-7 (pbk.)
  1. Stingrays—Juvenile literature. I. Title.
  QL638.8.Z45 2012
  597.3'5—dc23        2012001245

No part of this publication may be reproduced in whole or in part,
or stored in a retrieval system, or transmitted in any form or by any
means, electronic, mechanical, photocopying, recording, or otherwise,
without written permission of the publisher. For information regarding
permission, write to Scholastic Inc., Attention: Permissions Department,
557 Broadway, New York, NY 10012.
© 2013 Scholastic Inc.

All rights reserved. Published in 2013 by Children's Press, an imprint
of Scholastic Inc.
Printed in China 62
SCHOLASTIC, CHILDREN'S PRESS, and associated logos are
trademarks and/or registered trademarks of Scholastic Inc.

1 2 3 4 5 6 7 8 9 10 R 22 21 20 19 18 17 16 15 14 13

# Stingrays

| | |
|---|---|
| **Class** | Chondrichthyes |
| **Order** | Myliobatiformes |
| **Families** | Dasyatidae and Urolophidae |
| **Genus** | 9 genera |
| **Species** | Around 100 species |
| **World distribution** | All the world's oceans and some bodies of freshwater in South America and West Africa |
| **Habitats** | Warm temperate and tropical waters; most often found in shallow coastal areas; sometimes found in brackish water or freshwater |
| **Distinctive physical characteristics** | Wide, flat bodies formed by two large pectoral fins at either side of the head; two eyes on the top of the head, and a mouth and gill slits beneath; a long tail, usually with one or more spines |
| **Habits** | Spends most of its time on the seafloor, partially covered in sand; swims either by moving its pectoral fins in a wavelike motion or by flapping its fins like a bird; most species live alone but form groups during mating or migration |
| **Diet** | Worms, clams, oysters, crustaceans, and other invertebrates |

# Contents

# CHAPTER 1

# Serious Stingers

Have you ever seen a stingray? Stingrays have long tails and thin, wide bodies. They spend most of their time lying flat at the bottom of the ocean, partially covered in sand. Since a stingray's body is the same color as the ocean floor and it keeps very still, this fish is hard to see. It peeks its eyes up from the sand, watching out for possible threats. You might also spot a stingray gliding just above the sand, looking for food.

Stingrays are usually docile, or calm. Some **species** can even be friendly. But be careful not to step on one! A stingray can cause some serious damage if it thinks it is in danger. It will suddenly whip its tail up and use dangerous **spines** to stab at the threat.

Short-tail Stingray
14 ft. (4.3 m) wide

Adult Male
6 ft. (1.8 m)

Dwarf Whipray
9.4 in. (24 cm) wide

*Stingrays are a common sight along the sandy bottom of ocean beaches.*

6

# Flat Fish

A stingray's body is flat and wide. Some stingrays are shaped like diamonds or kites. Others are round like a pancake. The stingray's shape is largely formed by its pectoral fins. These fins stretch out to the stingray's sides from its head to its tail. The stingray's eyes are on top of its head. This allows it to keep an eye out for threats as it sits on the ocean floor. The stingray's mouth is on the bottom of its head, so it can pick up a tasty shrimp or oyster as it swims above. A stingray's tail is usually long and thin, with one or more poisonous spines. These stinging spines are what give the stingray its name.

**FUN FACT!** Beach visitors can avoid startling stingrays by shuffling their feet as they walk through the sand.

*A stingray's mouth is located on the bottom side of its wide, flat body.*

# Flexible Fins

Much like a shark, a stingray's skeleton has no bones. Instead, it is made entirely of cartilage. This is the same rubbery material that gives shape to people's noses and ears. This cartilaginous skeleton makes stingrays more flexible than most other animals. Vertebrates, including humans and fish, usually have at least some bones in their skeletons. Bones are hard. They cannot bend far without breaking.

The flexibility of caritlage allows stingrays to use their fins to get around. Most marine animals, such as sharks and dolphins, use their tails to move forward. Stingrays do not use their tails for swimming at all. Instead, most ripple the edges of their pectoral fins like waves. As the ripple moves from the front of the stingray's body to the back, it pushes the stingray forward. Other stingrays move around by flapping their fins up and down, much like a bird does with its wings.

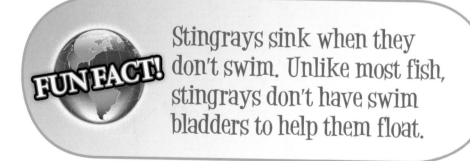

**FUN FACT!** Stingrays sink when they don't swim. Unlike most fish, stingrays don't have swim bladders to help them float.

*Stingrays can bend and twist their bodies.*

*Some stingrays
regularly shed and
regrow their spines.*

# CHAPTER 2

# Stingray Survival

Stingrays usually have one spine on their tails, though some species have two or more. Most spines are between 8 and 16 inches (20 and 40 centimeters) long. Stingrays only use their spines in defense. These weapons are designed to make a fast and effective attack so the stingray can escape. A stingray's spines are very sharp. This makes it easy for spines to become embedded in the flesh of the attacker. Some large stingrays are even strong enough to embed their spines in the side of a wooden boat. Most stingrays' spines also have serrated edges. These tiny ridges make it difficult for the attacker to pull the spine back out without causing even more damage.

Spines are a type of dermal denticle. Dermal denticles are made up of a strong material called dentin, which is the same material found on the inside of teeth. A stingray's scales are made of the same material. Spines and scales can grow back if they are lost.

*A stingray's deadly spine is located near the tip of its long tail.*

13

# A Serious Sting

In addition to the injury caused by the spine, venom can cause major damage to a stingray's enemies. The venom is located in grooves underneath and along the edges of the spine. Until the stingray attacks, the spine and its venom are protected by a thin sheath, or covering, on the stingray's tail. The sheath is pushed back as the spine enters the body of a potential predator. Once the spine pierces the enemy's skin, venom enters its bloodstream. Stingray venom can cause terrible pain or even paralysis. If a predator is distracted by pain or cannot move because of the venom, it poses no threat to the stingray. Some stingrays have venom that is strong enough to kill an attacker. Either way, the stingray has plenty of time to swim away.

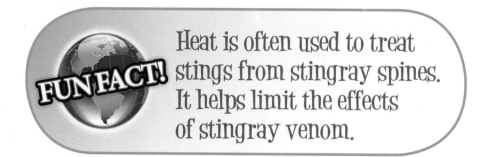

FUN FACT! Heat is often used to treat stings from stingray spines. It helps limit the effects of stingray venom.

*Even though stingrays are mostly peaceful, their tails can be incredibly deadly.*

# An Expert at Hiding

A stingray's thin body allows it to lie flat along the bottom of the ocean. Its coloring helps it blend in with its surroundings. Most stingrays are light or dark brown on top. This camouflage matches the colors of the surrounding sand. Stingrays that live in deeper waters are gray. Their dark coloring blends with the dark waters below. This hides them from predators looking down from above. Stingrays are white on the bottom. This hides them from prey swimming below them. The white blends in with the brighter, sunny waters above.

A stingray's camouflage also hides it from people. Sometimes people accidentally step on stingrays because they can't see the fish hiding beneath their feet. The stingrays defend themselves, not knowing that the people mean them no harm. Such attacks can cause serious injuries or even death. People are warned to be careful where they step when visiting areas where stingrays live.

*It can be very tough to spot a well-hidden stingray.*

# Breathing Underwater

Animals need oxygen to breathe. A stingray breathes by taking in water through holes called spiracles. Spiracles are located on top of the stingray's head. There is one behind each eye. Water flows into the spiracles and passes over the stingray's gills, which take oxygen from the water. Then the water passes out through gill slits. These are two holes located on the bottom of the stingray's head, near the mouth.

This method of breathing is different than that of most fish. Fish do not usually have spiracles. Instead, they take in water through their mouths. But stingrays spend a lot of time in the sand or swimming near the sandy floor. Their mouths, on the bottom of their heads, would only take in sand. Spiracles can take in more water because they are on top of the stingray's head, above the sand.

*Spiracles are large openings behind a stingray's eyes.*

# Electrical Hunting

Stingrays do not use their eyes to search for prey. Instead, they use special sensors called ampullae of Lorenzini. These tiny sensors are located in pores near the stingray's mouth. The pores lead to narrow, gel-filled canals in the stingray's skin. These canals lead to nerves that can sense the electrical fields of potential prey.

All animals naturally produce very small electrical fields. Fish and other marine animals produce stronger electrical fields when they use their gills. Stingrays use their ampullae to search for these electrical fields as they swim over the ocean or river floor. When the ampullae sense a nearby electrical field, the stingray can follow it to a tasty meal.

Scientists are still learning about ampullae of Lorenzini. Many scientists believe they can be used for more than just finding prey. Ampullae may also be used to sense the temperature, pressure, or saltiness of water.

*Ampullae of Lorenzini look like tiny spots on either side of a stingray's mouth.*

# CHAPTER 3

# Life Along the Sandy Floor

Stingrays are found in all the world's oceans. They mostly stick to tropical and warm temperate waters. Some common places to find them are in the waters surrounding Australia, the Americas, Asia, and parts of Africa. Most stingrays prefer the shallow waters along coastlines. Here, they can find plenty of food around coral reefs and other areas teeming with sea life. Some stingrays are found in open waters farther out to sea.

Stingrays sometimes venture into brackish water and freshwater, too. Atlantic stingrays have been found some 200 miles (322 kilometers) inland in the Mississippi River. Some species spend their whole lives in rivers. Many river rays are found in South America, mostly along the Amazon River and connecting rivers. Others live in Asia and West Africa.

*Stingrays are often found hiding in colorful coral reefs.*

# Dinnertime

Stingrays hunt for food along the ocean or river floor. Here, they find worms, crustaceans such as lobsters and crabs, oysters, clams, and other invertebrates. Most stingrays use their rows of interlocking teeth to crush the shells of their prey. This allows them to reach the animal's soft, nutritious inside.

Stingrays usually live independently of each other, but stingrays can gather together in groups in areas where there is plenty of food. They might line the ocean floor, hiding in the sand. They are also sometimes seen swimming together along the ocean floor in crowds. If a group of stingrays is large enough, it can completely wipe out an oyster or clam bed. This can cause problems for the surrounding ecosystem. Other animals, such as seabirds, that depend on oysters or clams for food go hungry. This affects animals that depend on seabirds, as well as the other animals up and down the food chain.

*Stingrays dig into the sand to hunt for tasty treats.*

# Stingray Pups

Outside of feeding time, the only reason stingrays gather together is to mate. A stingray mates only once each year. Much like other fish, stingray babies, called pups, grow inside eggs before being born. But unlike most other egg layers, stingrays are ovoviviparous. This means that the eggs stay inside the mother until after the pups have hatched. This might take anywhere from four months to a year. After hatching, the pups are born live. The hatchlings are rolled up tightly like cigars at first. They unroll their tails and fins as they enter the ocean. A mother usually gives birth to a litter of two to six pups.

Pups are almost fully developed when they are born. They enter the world with tails, fins, and heads much like their parents, only smaller. They can find food and defend themselves. Because of this, pups are left to take care of themselves at birth.

**FUN FACT!** Small fish and shrimps at reef "cleaning stations" clean stingrays and other fish of algae, bacteria, and other harmful materials.

*Newborn stingrays are very small.*

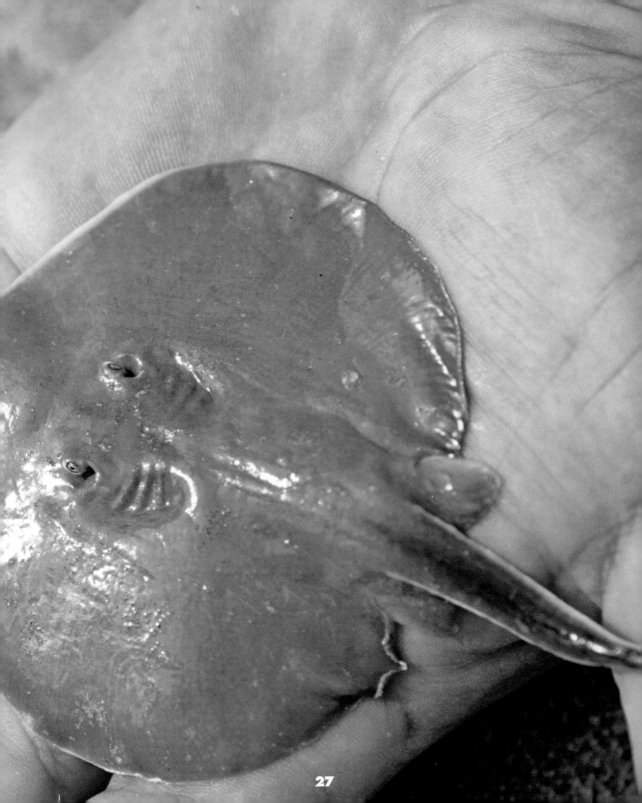

23

# CHAPTER 4

# Stingrays Through History

Humans have known about stingrays for thousands of years. Ancient Greeks wrote about epic heroes who were killed by weapons made from a stingray's tail spine. In 1608, English explorer John Smith nearly died trying to capture a stingray near the Jamestown colony in Virginia. For centuries, soldiers and hunters around the world have used stingray tail spines as weapons. Native groups all across the Americas put them on the tips of spears. The sharp, poisonous spines made these weapons even more dangerous.

Tales of stingrays were not all bad. Some people once believed that stingray livers had healing properties. Ancient Greek doctors used stingray venom to help ease pain. Today, scientists are studying stingrays to try to find new treatments for certain diseases in humans.

*A stingray spine was used in making this weather charm from the Caroline Islands. The charm was believed to ward off storms.*

# An Undecided Family Tree

Stingrays first developed around 200 million years ago. This was during the time of the dinosaurs. Over time, stingrays diversified into the 100 or so species known today.

Scientists disagree about whether stingrays should all be grouped into one family or separated into two. The main stingray family is Dasyatidae. These stingrays are found all over the world. They can grow to be quite large. One species stretches to about 7 feet (2 meters) wide and 14 feet (4 m) long on average. Stingrays of the Dasyatidae family have long, whiplike tails, earning them the nickname whip-tailed rays.

Round stingrays are sometimes grouped together with the Dasyatidae, but some scientists give them their own family, Urolophidae. These stingrays are much smaller than others, usually growing no larger than 23 inches (58 cm) long. Their tails are short and stout. Round rays are most often found in the waters around North America.

*Round stingrays have dangerous spines, but they lack the long tails of their relatives.*

# Close Ray Relatives

Stingrays are not the only kind of rays. Other ray species can be found almost anywhere in the world, from deep oceans to shallow riverbeds. Some have tail spines, much like stingrays. These species include eagle rays, cow-nosed rays, and some butterfly rays. Others have no tail spine at all and are considered harmless. However, rays do not need spines to be impressive.

The manta ray can weigh more than 3,000 pounds (1,360 kilograms) and reach widths of more than 20 feet (6 m). Two cephalic fins stick out from the front of a manta ray's head. Because these fins can look like horns, the manta ray is sometimes also known as the devil ray. Unlike any other ray species, the manta ray can leap above the water's surface. Mantas have been seen leaping 9 feet (2.7 m) or more into the air. They can twist and turn and sometimes do somersaults, entering the water headfirst.

**FUN FACT!** Some rays' tails are long enough to hit an attacker located directly in front of the ray.

*Manta rays look as if they are flying when they leap from the water.*

# Skates, Saws, and Sharks

Skates look a lot like rays. Their bodies are flat and wide, with two large pectoral fins and a long tail. Like rays, they are bottom feeders. But skates never birth live pups. Instead, they lay eggs in special cases called mermaid's purses.

The sawfish is a stranger-looking relative of the stingray. As its name implies, a sawfish is born with a sawlike snout on the front of its face. This snout sticks out like a long, barbed nose. A sawfish's snout is made of specialized dermal denticles, like a stingray's tail spine.

Skates, sawfish, and rays are very closely related to sharks. In fact, the first rays may have looked more like modern sharks than modern rays. Like stingrays, sharks are members of the Chondrichthyes class. This means they have skeletons made of cartilage. But these fish don't just sit in the sand like rays do. They swim through shallow waters or the open ocean, hunting down fish, squid, and other sea creatures for dinner.

*A sawfish's incredible nose sets it apart from its relatives.*

# CHAPTER 5

# Dangerous Waters

Most stingray species are not described as **endangered**. For some species, this is because scientists do not have enough information to track their numbers. For other species, scientists know that there are plenty to be found in the wild. However, this could soon change.

Dangerous chemicals are a common part of industry, farming, and other human activities. These chemicals often make their way into sewer drains, streams, and rivers, or are soaked into the ground. Here, they kill off plants and poison animals. If too many plants or animals die, other animals can lose a food source. The chemicals can also cause health problems in water animals. Because stingrays live so close to shore, they are heavily affected. Some species are already in danger of disappearing. Scientists worry that more will follow.

*Scientists still have a lot to learn about many stingray species.*

# In the Rivers and Estuaries

Few stingray species are currently considered endangered. One is the Mekong freshwater stingray. It lives in the Mekong River basin in Southeast Asia, between Cambodia and Thailand. Over the last 20 years, this stingray's population has decreased by half. This is partially due to chemicals being dumped into its home rivers. The species also suffers from fishing. Fishers often catch the stingrays by accident. More damage is caused when people build dams along the Mekong River. This makes it more difficult for the stingrays to travel to find food or to mate.

The other stingray that is considered endangered is the daisy stingray. This stingray is found along the West African coast and nearby islands. Most live in ocean and brackish waters around the shore. Like the Mekong freshwater stingray, the daisy stingray suffers from overfishing. Over the past several years, the species has become harder and harder to find.

*The endangered giant freshwater whipray is also found in the Mekong River basin.*

# Protecting the Future

Several other stingray species are listed as near threatened. The situation is made worse by major disasters, such as oil spills. For example, the 2010 Deepwater Horizon oil spill caused huge losses in marine life in the Gulf of Mexico. Currently, there are no laws to specifically protect stingrays, but many conservationists are working to change this.

Scientists gain more knowledge about stingrays every year. This knowledge helps them understand how human activity affects these fish. Many scientists travel around the world to study stingrays in the wild. Sometimes, stingrays are captured and brought to zoos and aquariums. There, everyone can get a peek at stingray life. Many scientists use these facilities as an opportunity to spread the word about stingray protection. With everyone's help, these remarkable fish can have a bright future.

*Aquariums and marine parks offer people a chance to get up close and personal with stingrays.*

# Words to Know

ampullae of Lorenzini (AM-pyoo-lye UV lor-en-ZEE-nee) — specialized organs used to sense electrical waves

brackish (BRAK-ish) — water that is saltier than freshwater but not as salty as seawater

camouflage (KAM-o-flaj) — coloring or body shape that allows an animal to blend in with its surroundings

cartilage (KAR-tih-lidj) — tough elastic tissue

cephalic fins (seh-FA-lik FINZ) — fins attached to the head of certain animals

conservationists (kon-sur-VAY-shuhn-ists) — people who work to protect an environment and the living things in it

crustaceans (krus-TAY-shunz) — animals such as shrimp, crabs, lobsters, and crayfish that have jointed legs, hard shells, and no backbones

dermal denticle (DUR-muhl DEN-tih-kul) — specialized tiny structure found on the skin that is made of material similar to teeth

diversified (di-VUR-si-fide) — grew differently

ecosystem (EE-koh-sis-tuhm) — all the living things in a place and their relation to the environment

endangered (en-DAYN-jurd) — at risk of becoming extinct, usually because of human activity

family (FAM-uh-lee) — a group of living things that are related to each other

food chain (FOOD CHAYN) — an ordered arrangement of animals and plants in which each feeds on the one below it on the chain

gills (GILZ) — organs that remove oxygen from water to help fish and other underwater animals breathe

invertebrates (in-VUR-tuh-brits) — animals without a backbone

mate (MAYT) — to join together to produce babies

ovoviviparous (OH-voh-vye-VIH-puh-russ) — describing animals whose young hatch from eggs inside the mother, then are born live

paralysis (puh-RAL-i-sis) — a loss of power to move or feel a part of the body

pectoral (PEK-tuh-ruhl) — toward an animal's chest or the front of its body

pores (PORZ) — tiny holes in the skin

predator (PREH-duh-tur) — an animal that lives by hunting other animals for food

prey (PRAY) — an animal that's hunted by another animal for food

serrated (sehr-A-ted) — having a jagged edge

species (SPEE-sheez) — one of the groups into which animals and plants of the same genus are divided

spines (SPINES) — sharp, pointy structures at the end of a stingray's tail

spiracles (SPEER-ik-uhlz) — openings in certain animals to take in water or air to breathe

temperate (TEM-pur-it) — having a climate where the temperature is rarely very high or very low

threatened (THRET-uhnd) — at risk of becoming endangered

venom (VEH-num) — poison produced by some animals

vertebrates (VER-tuh-bruts) — animals that have a backbone

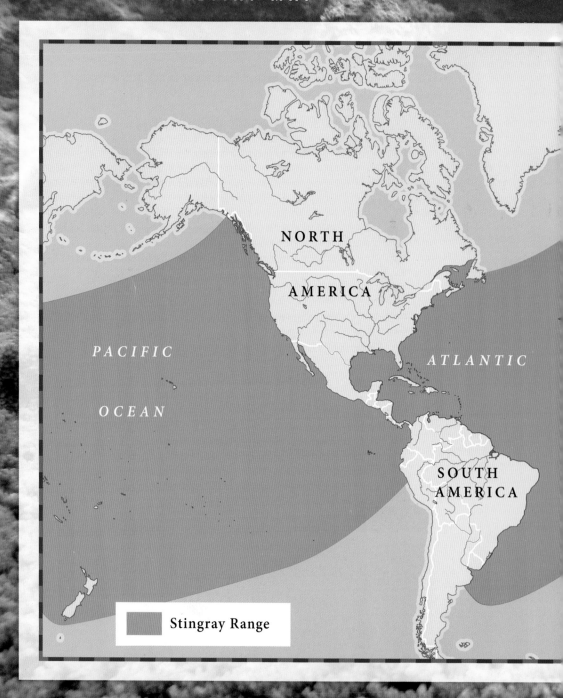

NORTH

AMERICA

PACIFIC

OCEAN

*ATLANTIC*

SOUTH
AMERICA

Stingray Range

ARCTIC OCEAN

EUROPE

ASIA

AFRICA

PACIFIC OCEAN

OCEAN

INDIAN

OCEAN

AUSTRALIA

# Find Out More

Books

Gross, Miriam J. *The Stingray*. New York: PowerKids Press, 2006.

Walker, Sally M. *Rays*. Minneapolis: Carolrhoda Books, 2003.

Wearing, Judy. *Manta Rays*. New York: Weigl Publishers, 2010.

Visit this Scholastic Web site for more information on stingrays:
**www.factsfornow.scholastic.com**
Enter the keyword **Stingrays**

# Index

# About the Author

Jennifer Zeiger lives in Chicago, Illinois, where she writes and edits books for children. She has always been interested in stingrays. She even got to pet some at the Aquarium of the Pacific in Long Beach, California!